My First Amazing Mazes
Animal Mazes

HIGHLIGHTS PRESS
Honesdale, Pennsylvania

The Way Home

It's time for baby Belle to come home.
Can you help her find a path to her mother?

Finish

Kite Strings

Draw a kite at the end of each string. Then follow each string to find out which animal is holding which kite.

Baby Elephant

Eli wants to catch up with his momma. Can you help him find a path back to her?

Safari Race

It's time for a refreshing dip! Follow each path to help the animals get to the watering hole.

Art by Anna Jones

Porcupine Problems

Penelope is meeting her friends at the state fair. Can you help her find a path through the balloons to her friends?

Start

Finish

PRIZES

Time for Bed

Did you know koalas can sleep up to 22 hours a day? Follow each path to find where each koala sleeps.

A Day at the Park

It's a beautiful day at the park! Follow each path to connect each squirrel to its match.

Art by Jan Bryan-Hunt

Downhill Slope

Bear and his friends are going sledding. Can you help Bear find a path to the bottom?

Hat Party

Time to play dress up! Follow each path to see which hat each hedgehog will wear.

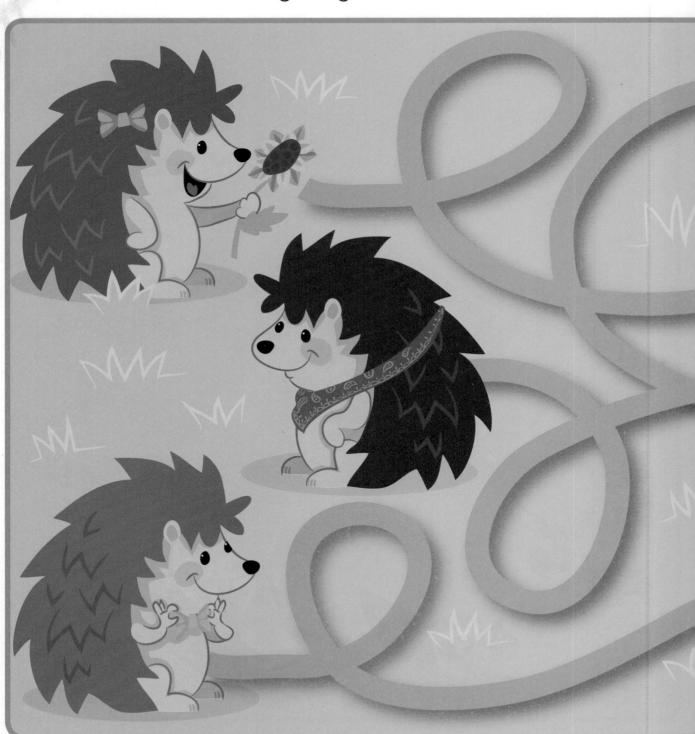

Lost Stripes

Baby Zadie lost her momma. Can you follow the Z's and help her find a path back to her mother?

Early Bird

These birds are trying to catch their breakfast. Follow each path to find out which bird gets the worm.

Art by Adam Record

Ant-Hill Tunnels

Andy's friends are leaving without him! Can you help him find a path out of the anthill?

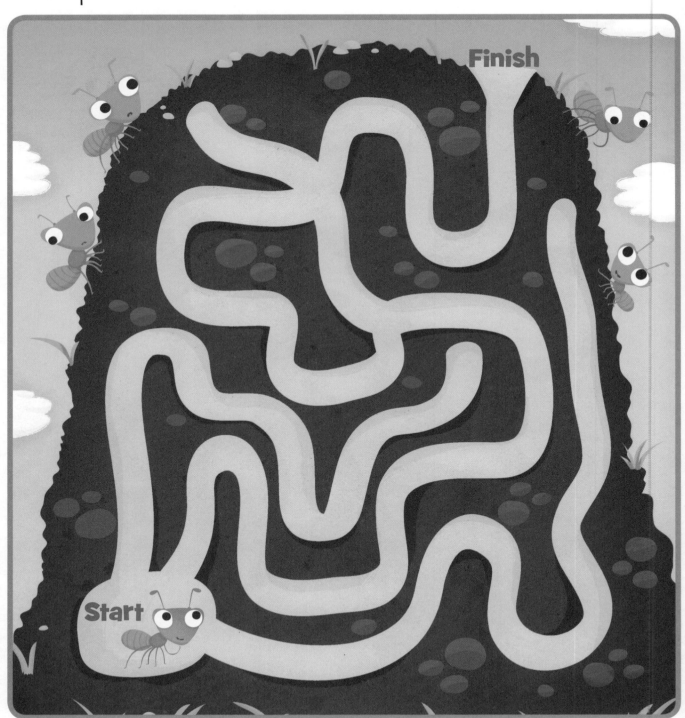

Art by Mattia Cerato

Jellyfish Jumble

Jamie wants to join his friends. Can you follow the J's and help him find a path to them?

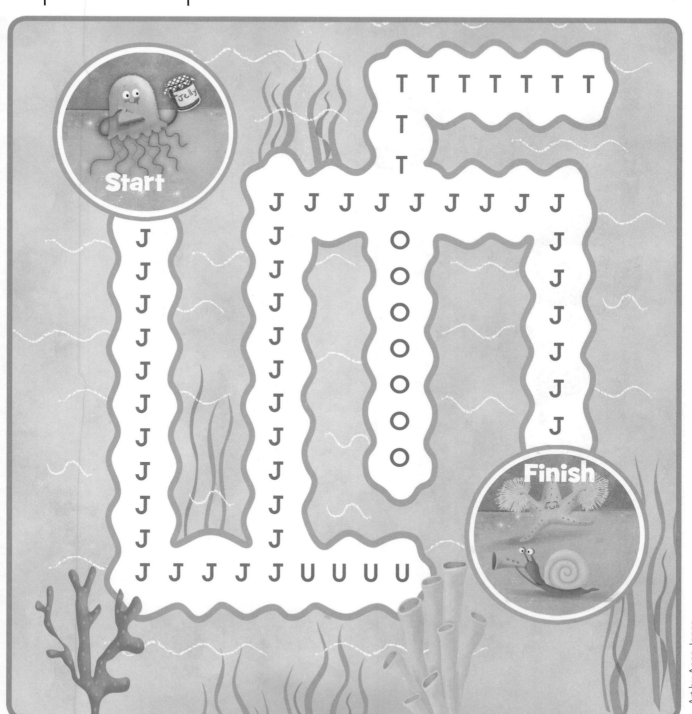

Art by Anna Jones

Skate Race

These three bears are having a race. Follow each path to see which bear will win the race.

Art by Kevin Zimmer

Flower Landing

Spring is in the air! Follow each path to see which flower each bug will land on.

Splish Splash

Leo is ready to join his friends! Can you help him find a path to the pool?

Ocean Dive

Dolly thinks it's a great day for a swim! Can you help her find a path to her friend?

Finish

Meow Maze

Can you help the mouse get to the cheese?
Be sure to stay away from the cats!

Llama Mama

This llama needs his mama! Can you help the baby llama find a path to her?

Finish

Ollie's Garden

Oscar is meeting his friend Ollie. Can you help him find a path to Ollie's garden?

Art by Brian Fitzgerald

Prairie Dog Days

These prairie dogs are heading home. Follow each tunnel to see which burrow belongs to each prairie dog.

Art by Debbie Palen

Bamboo Forest

Perry wants to eat bamboo with his friend. Can you help him find a clear path through the bamboo forest?

Art by Hazel Quintanilla

Catching Waves

Shawn and his friends are out catching some gnarly waves! Follow each path to see who makes it to the shore first.

Art by Kelly Kennedy

Farm Tails

Kit wandered away from her family. Can you help her find a path back to them?

Start

Finish

Fetch!

Buster is trying to sniff his way to the dog park. Can you help him find a path?

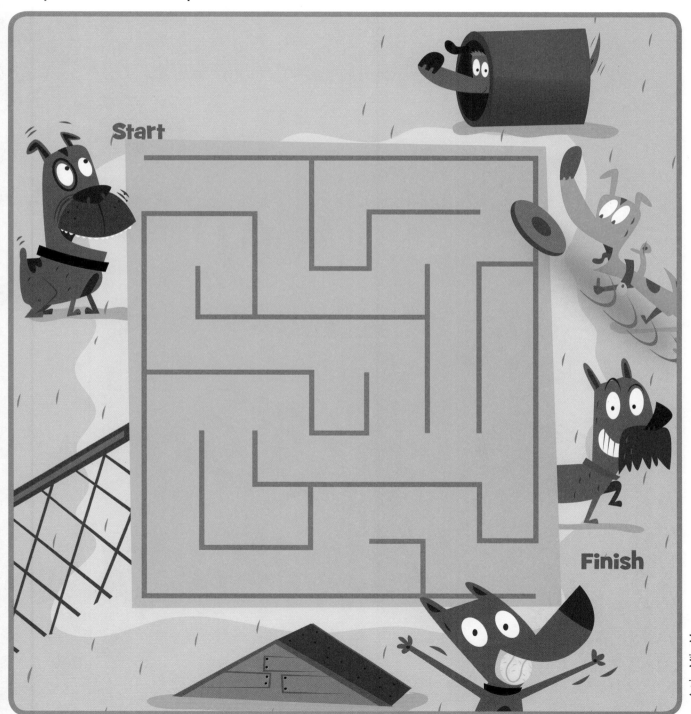

Sloth Sleuthing

Sherlock is conducting an investigation.
Can you help him find a path to the evidence?

Finish

Pet Store Mania

These pets are getting spoiled today! Follow each path to see what each pet got from the pet store.

Barnyard Living

Ottie is returning home for a nap. Follow the path to see where he lives.

Art by Rocco Baviera

Kitty Toys

These kittens love to play! Follow each path to see which toy belongs to which kitten.

Animal Homes

Bert is heading back to the hive.
Can you help him find a path back home?

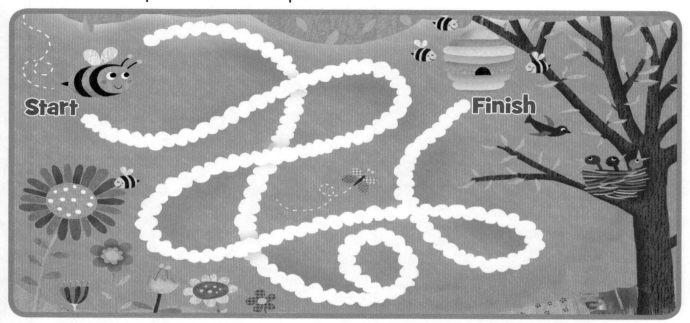

Beverly needs to get back to work. Can you help her find a path to the river?

Strike!

There's always chaos at the Armadillo Alley. Follow each path to see which bowler knocked down the most pins.

Rise and Shine!

Gary needs to wake up! Can you help the sleepy groundhog find a path outside?

Sam is collecting acorns for winter. Can you help the hungry squirrel find a path to the acorns?

Tongue Tied

These frogs mixed up their lunches. Follow the tongues to find out what each frog caught.

Art by Shelley Brant

Dance Maze

Hector wants to ask Hilda to dance. Can you help him find a clear path to her?

Finish

Chickie Come Home

Chick is late for naptime! Can you help her get back to her coop by following the pattern? ●▲●▲

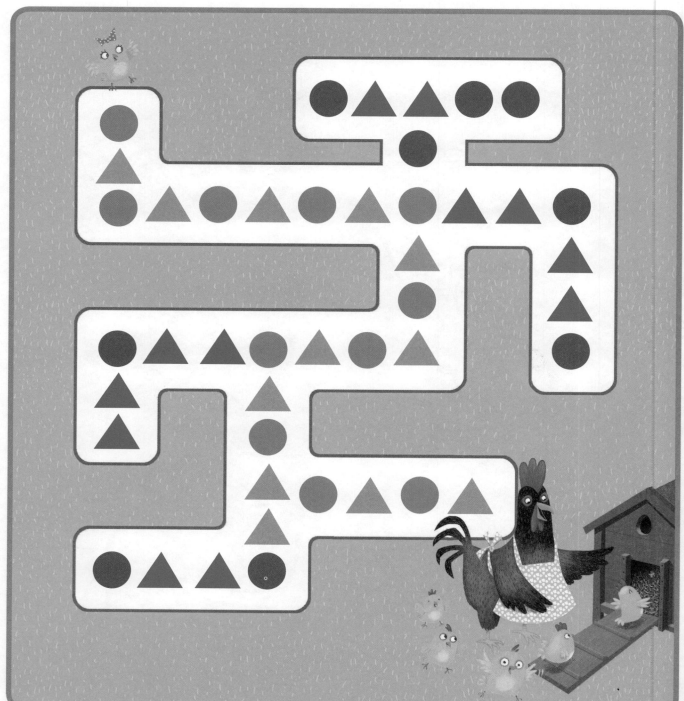

Crab Walk

Carl is trying to get back to the ocean. Can you help him find a path to the water?

Start

Finish

Art by Mattia Cerato

Answers

Pages 2-3

Page 4

Page 5

Page 6

Page 7

Pages 8-9

Page 10
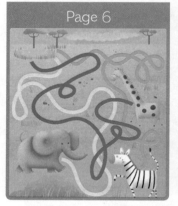

Page 11

Pages 12-13

Page 14

Page 15

Page 16

Page 17

Answers

Pages 18-19

Page 20

Page 21

Pages 22-23

Page 24

Page 25

Page 26

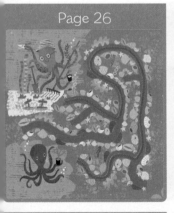

Page 27

Page 28

Page 29

Page 30

Page 31

Pages 32-33

Answers

Page 34

Page 35

Page 36

Page 37

Pages 38-39

Page 40

Page 41

Pages 42-43

Page 44

Page 45

For information about permission to reproduce selections from this book, please contact permissions@highlights.com.

Published by Highlights Press
815 Church Street
Honesdale, Pennsylvania 18431
ISBN: 978-1-68437-259-1
Manufactured in Guangzhou, Guangdong, China
Mfg. 07/2019

First edition
Visit our website at Highlights.com.
10 9 8 7 6 5 4 3 2

Cover art by Constanza Basaluzzo

little blue and little yellow

a story for Pippo and Ann
and other children
by Leo Lionni

HarperCollinsPublishers

Library of Congress Cataloging-in-Publication Data
Lionni, Leo.
  Little blue and little yellow / Leo Lionni.
      p.   cm.
  Summary: A little blue spot and a little yellow spot are best friends, and when they
hug each other they become green.
  ISBN 0-688-13285-5
  [1. Color—Fiction.   2. Friendship—Fiction.]   I. Title.
PZ7.L6634Li   1995   94-7324
[E]—dc20   CIP
                                                                                        AC

Visit us on the World Wide Web!
www.harperchildrens.com
10 11 12 13 SCP 30 29 28 27 26 25 24

This is little blue.

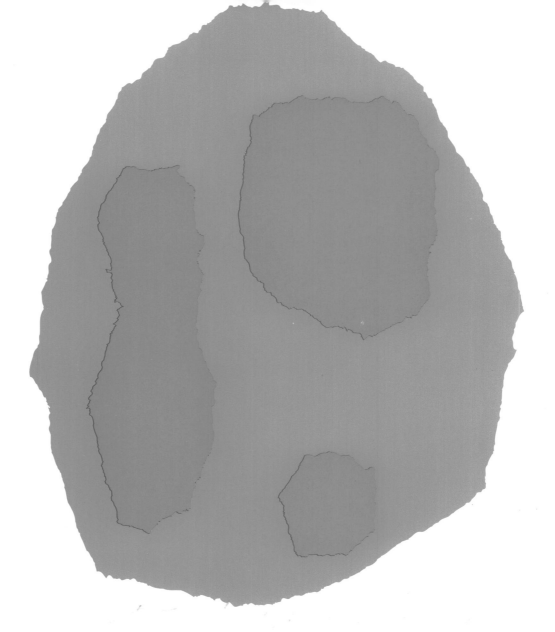

Here he is at home with papa and mama blue.

Little blue has many friends

but his best friend is little yellow

who lives across the street.

How they love to play at *Hide-and-Seek*

and *Ring-a-Ring-O' Roses!*

In school they sit still in neat rows.

After school they run and jump.

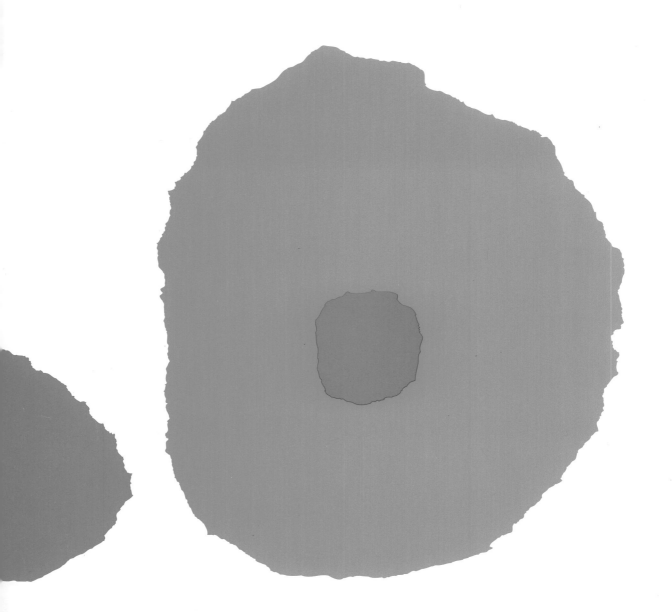

One day mama blue went shopping. "You stay home" she said to little blue.

But little blue went out to look for little yellow.

Alas! The house across the street was empty.

He looked here

and there

and everywhere...until suddenly, around a corner

there was little yellow!

Happily they hugged each other

and hugged each other

until they were green.

Then they went to play in the park.

They ran through a tunnel.

They chased little orange.

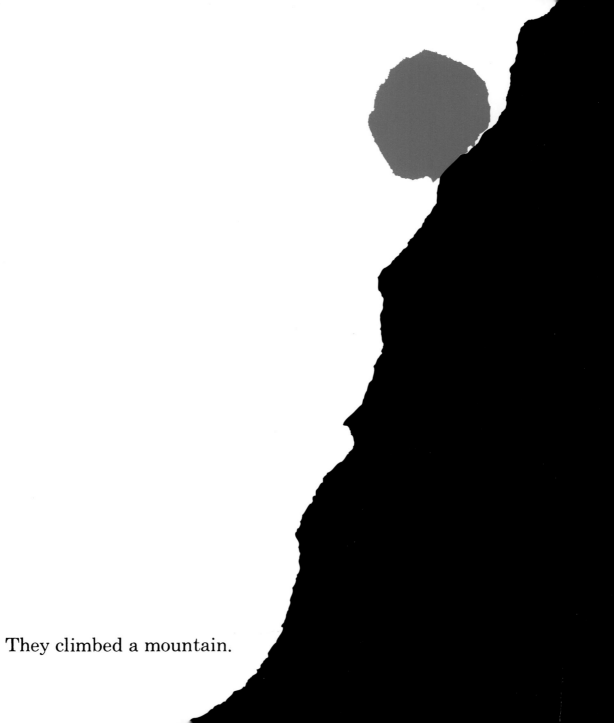

They climbed a mountain.

When they were tired

they went home.

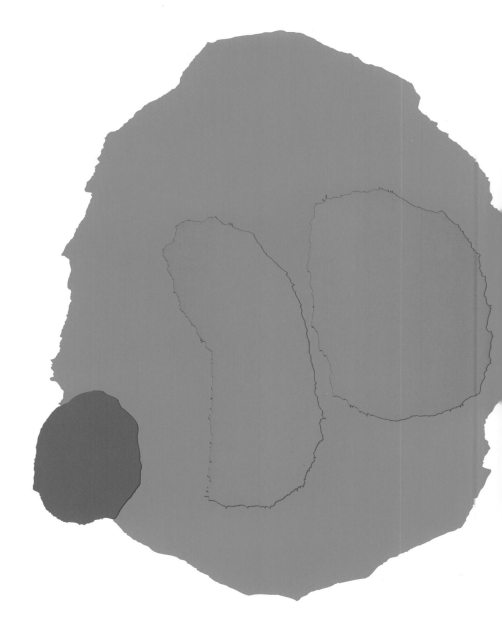

But papa and mama blue said: "You are not our little blue—you are green."

And papa and mama yellow said: "You are not our little yellow—you are green."

Little blue and little yellow were very sad. They cried big blue and yellow tears

They cried and cried until they were *all* tears.

When they finally pulled themselves together they said: "Will they
                                                            believe us
                                                            now?"

Mama blue and papa blue were very happy to see their little blue.

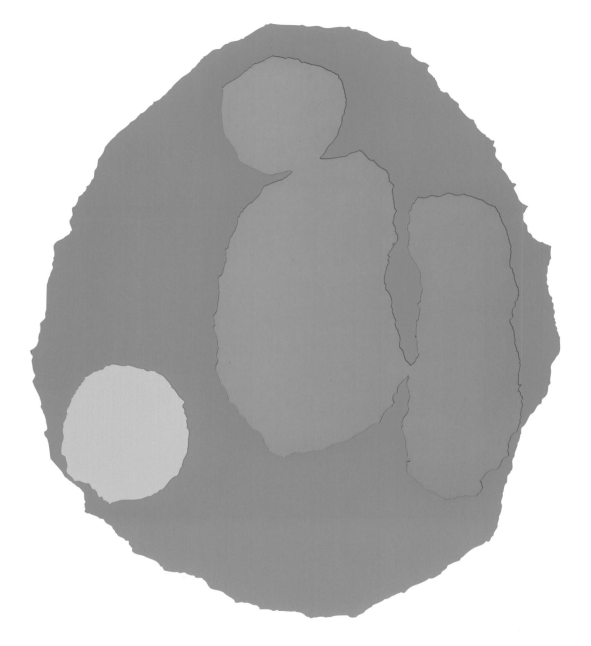

They hugged and kissed him

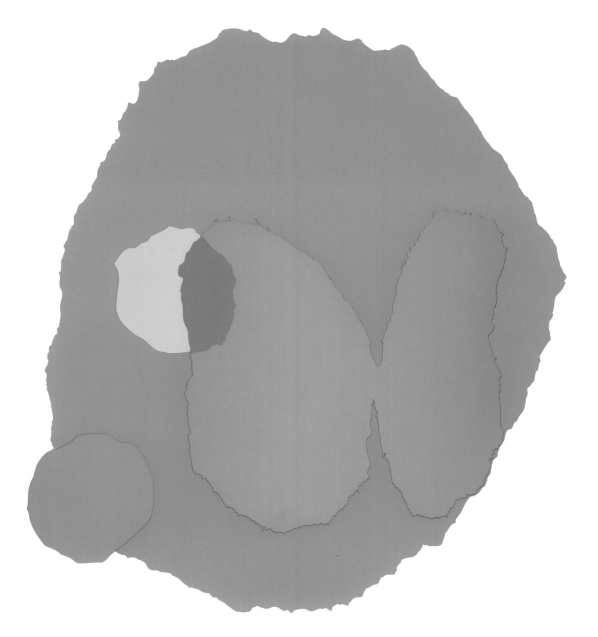

And they hugged little yellow too...but look . . . they became green!

Now they knew what had happened

and so they went across the street to bring the good news.

They all hugged each other with joy

and the children played until suppertime.

The End

More Picture Books
by Leo Lionni

Inch by Inch. A winning, winsome inchworm is proud of his ability to measure just about anything under the sun— and then some. (ISBN 0-688-13283-9)

On My Beach There Are Many Pebbles. Challenge young readers to look closely at the most ordinary of objects to discover the extraordinary beauty and majesty of each. (ISBN 0-688-13284-7)